The Abyss

~

David Ruffle

Paperback ISBN 978-1-78092-547-9
ePub ISBN 978-1-78092-548-6
PDF ISBN 978-1-78092-549-3

Published in the UK by MX Publishing
335 Princess Park Manor, Royal Drive, London, N11 3GX

www.mxpublishing.com

Cover layout and construction by
www.staunch.com

Also by David Ruffle

Sherlock Holmes and the Lyme Regis Horror

Sherlock Holmes and the Lyme Regis Horror (expanded 2nd Edition)

Sherlock Holmes and the Lyme Regis Legacy

Holmes and Watson: End Peace

Sherlock Holmes and the Lyme Regis Trials

For Children

Sherlock Holmes and the Missing Snowman

(illustrated by Rikey Austin)

As editor and contributor

Tales from the Stranger's Room (Vol.1)

Tales from the Stranger's Room (Vol. 2)

2

By the pricking of my thumbs…
something wicked this way comes.
- *Macbeth, Act 4, Scene 1.*

Whoever fights monsters should see
to it that he does not become a monster
in the process. And if you gaze long enough
into the abyss, the abyss will gaze back into you.

-Friedrich Nietzche

3

Some of the following happened, some of it did not. Or you could say most of it happened, but some did not. Or you could say that some of it or indeed most of it happened, but not in this way. Although it could have happened in this way, or some of it at least.

He has seen the abyss. It is waiting. Welcoming and inviting.

The voices, now more nagging and insistent propel him forward. His last shreds of resistance are used up. He is resigned, even calm you might say. The steady stream of early morning human traffic crossing the bridge would counter this, for they see a deranged madman in their midst. A man in the throes of uttering a silent scream with hands over his ears, clawing wildly at his hair. They move on quickly, not wishing to play any part in this drama being played out in front of them.

He suddenly stands quite still as if he is only now aware of where he is; the bridge; the abyss.

The voices close in.

DEFINITIONS

a·byss (uh-bis)

Noun

1. a deep, immeasurable space, gulf, or cavity; vast chasm.

2. anything profound, unfathomable, or infinite: the abyss of time.

3. a. the primal chaos before Creation.

   b. the infernal regions; hell.

   c. a subterranean ocean.

ONE

The abyss was always waiting of course. It began to open up in the void of his childhood where the patterns of all our lives are set. His fate; to be born of staunchly religious parents. His fate; to live in a house of darkness, repression and fear. Even the very fabric of the house itself taunted him, with its dark corners and cold walls. Discipline was harsh and punishments meted out with a barely disguised glee. The merest slip when reciting a passage from the Bible was enough to merit 'the rod'. A word out of place was deserving of a beating. What resistance can there be when you are so young? Perhaps, he wondered one day, that this life is normal, for he had no siblings or friends with whom he could compare daily life. Even as a child he learned to control the pain he felt and quickly learned too that tears were a weakness that demanded yet more punishment. Emotions became dulled.

He knew little of the world outside. His parents took no newspapers and the only reading material in the house was the Bible. A huge, heavy bible with a metal clasp which left an imprint on his young skin many a time. He knew nothing of schooling, had not and was not prepared for it. How he remembers that morning. His mother dressing him in his Sunday best and marching him through the unfamiliar village and depositing him outside the school gates with scarcely a word. Scared? Of course. The urge to run, to escape was strong, but there was nowhere to go. When he looked at the other children, he knew he was different. They knew it too. They spoke of mushroom picking, of conkers, of games he did not know and could not share in. He came from another world, he knew it. They knew it too. The taunting started then, the teasing, the bullying. Pain became the norm in school as at home. It scarcely improved matters when it became apparent he was a very apt pupil. Achieving top marks in nearly every subject opened up new avenues in the remorseless bullying. Of course, the mysterious accident which befell the bullies' ringmaster all but put an end to that. Just how he stumbled into the path of the horse and cart was never really established. The locals uttered the usual warnings about children larking about on the streets. Timothy Breakspear eventually returned to school, but his potency to cajole others into doing his dirty work for him was compromised by the mere fact of his only now having one leg. He instead, elicited pity from all the children. Save one. Who smiled at him in a way that chilled young Master Breakspear to the bone.

The school had a reasonably sized library and while the other children went through their twice daily routine of inane games on the playground, he read, he studied. He devoured adventurous lives that he would never have. He read of countries and cities he would never visit save in his imagination. This was his secret world. A world where he could not be harmed. An hour's reading a day was not enough to sate his curiosity so he began a campaign of judicious smuggling of books home under his blazer. Discovery was swift, punishment swifter still. The small congregation in the chapel his parents belonged to were told of his wickedness. Pray for James, they were urged, lest he be lost to us. They duly prayed. The headmaster, who also was a chapel goer, decided that the best policy was to close the library during the children's play time. A more permanent closure of the library was forced upon the school when fire tore through the room, destroying the entire stock. Blame was apportioned to the caretaker who was dismissed from his post. It seems he had been in the habit of smoking a cigarette in the library whilst neglecting his duties. So, one child reported anyway. That was the last of the misfortunes to befall the Breakspear family other than the fact that neither father nor son would ever find gainful employment.

The winter of 1859/60 was the coldest in living memory. The biting chill winds roared in from the east for month after long month. The school closed for the whole of January and although the normality of village life was suspended, life at home was depressingly normal. And yet it wasn't. His father had become a travelling lay-preacher and was absent for much of the time. During that freezing January he was becalmed in Norfolk, from where missives would flow exhorting his dear wife to be firm with James as he would be himself if he was there. This she took to heart. With relish. His mother decreed that there would be an hour's bible reading every night until father came home. For this, he was expected to learn by rote, several pages and recite them word for word whilst sitting on the rug in front of the fire. Should he have difficulty remembering, the poker was on hand as an aid to memory. His mother may have been a frail woman but religious fervour gave strength to her arm that few would credit. Such were the long winter evenings until an act of carelessness on his mother's part resulted in her dress catching fire. Although it took some time to find the bucket of water which normally stood in the corner of the scullery, for it had unaccountably been moved, James was able to extinguish the flames before his mother suffered a serious injury. Bed rest was the advice of the doctor. A letter was despatched to his father which only reached him two weeks later in Hunstanton. Neighbours and chapel goers looked in and supplied meals. There were offers to take James in for the duration, but he protested that he wanted to stay close to his mother and the offers were withdrawn. Besides, nobody really wanted to take him in. He was odd, they said, a little touched. He heard the whispers. He was different, he knew it. They knew it too.

He had seen the boys at school with their home-made catapults, directing their missiles at targets such as old bottles and cans. Now seemed the perfect time to create one for himself. You could hardly call the finished product a thing of beauty, yet it felt good to him to hold it in his hand, its rough edges perfectly suited to his virgin grip. He spent a full hour in the garden hunting down rounded pebbles. In the end he had a collection of at least one hundred, shiny and perfect. The novelty of shooting off flower petals soon expired and he looked around for a different target, one which demanded greater skill and accuracy. Of course, he should have known, the solution was there all the time. Birds. Enticed with scraps from the larder placed on the bird table, they would make the perfect targets. Standing on an upturned bucket enabled him to reach the table, the grazed knees only heightened the thrill of adventure. It took some little while to get the hang of aiming at a moving target, but he was rewarded with the sight of the first bird to fall, a sparrow. More followed. If they survived the fall, well there were ways that could be devised to hasten their departure from the world. Was that when he first entered the abyss?

TWO-ONE

Five shillings, I mean what bleedin' good was that? That Billy was always tight with his money, should 'ave done better for meself and that's a fact dears. Cruel man too, always throwing me out. And there was me so bloody weak and feeble that I always went back. Billy boy, you might 'ave well 'ave done me in yourself. A misery he was, a right misery. Lawd knows what that so called, good for nothing midwife saw in him. Angels of mercy? Don't get me started. You'll be alright Polly, don't worry 'bout a thing she says and when I was asleep wiv being tired of lookin' after little Eliza she is upstairs wiv 'him, bold as brass. Five shillings, what was I supposed to do, you tell me that dear. You'll 'ave me in the workhouse I told 'im. Billy don't care about that Mary said an' she was right an' all. Even turned me Dad against me, he did. All that was before that floozy came along. Is any wonder that I 'ad to 'ave the occasional gin to steady meself like. Medicinal you could say even. He used to say it put fight in me. I could handle meself alright. I was strong-armed like Dad. The neighbour children around Shoe Lane would queue up to be paraded around hangin' from Dad's arms like washing on the line. I see you are lookin' at my scar, that's where it came from you see. I was just a little mite an' jumped onto Dad's arm from the 'all table. Hey gal look out he said as he swung me around an' around till I bashed me 'ead on the door frame. Bled everywhere it did, all down me face and onto me smock. Ma cut up rough about that she did as she 'ad only just washed an' dried it. We was schooled best we could. All us kids in Dawes Court went round the corner to St.Marys, can't say as it

11

did any of us any good like, we were not the learnin' type. We 'ad each other to learn from in our rough an' tumble play. Well I guess some learnin' must 'ave got inside our skulls not that girls were meant to learn, oh no, not the likes of us anyway. All we were fit for was marryin' and 'aving kids of our own. Nice little gal you got there George, make someone a good wife someday, they used to say. A good wife, what a laugh. Billy lived round the corner and took a right old shine to me 'e did. 'E never took liberties wiv me, well, I wouldn't let him would I. Anyway, we found ourselves married and me only nineteen at that. Poor sap never 'ad no money either, called 'imself a skilled machinist if you please, but that meant nothin' to me. An' then the kids came along all five of 'em. Good kids mind, but they drove me to blessed distraction. Fair wore me out they did. An' to cap it all we was back livin' wiv me Dad. Not that 'e minded having his grandkids around and it gave me the chance to get out and about so to speak. Beer was me tipple then, London ale was cheap if you knew where to go an' believe me I did me dears. Billy an' the kids, well they was alright. Me or me Dad fed them, specially Dad when I was a touch unwell. Funny ain't it, can 'ardly remember their faces now. Peabody Buildings, 'ated living there, an 'ovel that's what it was an' we 'ad to pay 5/6d for the rent. Bleedin' 5/6d I ask you. Of course it was when we was there that Billy got up to 'is tricks wiv the nurse an' I 'ad to get out. Now don't you listen to folk who say that Billy threw me out on account of me drinkin' too much. That's stuff and nonsense put about by people wiv too much time on their 'ands and lookin' for gossip to fill their empty 'eads wiv. Anyway I cleared off and lived off my wits and slept 'ere and there always finding money for the price of a bed if you know what I mean. I was down on me luck a few times mind an' Lambeth workhouse took me in. Bleedin' bloody Lambeth workhouse, do you know what they did? Only found me some oh so respectable people to go 'an work for. Lawd above,

12

they was even teetotallers, not a drop of drink in the 'ouse, well I mean to say, it ain't natural is it. Anyway, dears, that was later on after I met Tom. Big strong man was Tom, a bit like me dad. 'E wanted to settle down all domestic like there above 'is shop in Walworth. Walworth, it ain't Kensington is it now. Let's 'ave kids he says. You 'ave kids I say, I've 'ad mine. Cleared off again didn't I, back to me life on the streets, Those workhouses kept takin' me in, wantin' to reform me I guess. Like I was sayin' I ended up as a maid of all things, me who couldn't tell one end of a broom from another. I put up wiv it for two months all those holier than thou graces of the precious Cowdry's an' then upped sticks an' scarpered out of it. Pinched some clothes too, not to wear me dears, but to sell, not that I got much for 'em. An' then got meself into Grays Inn workhouse for a few weeks until I got meself back on my feet or on me back if you will excuse me language, but I was what I was an' what else could I do to rake in a few pennies. Lawd knows there was no pleasure in it for me, mind you between me you and the bed post there weren't any pleasure in it in me marriage bed either, dears. But like I says what else could I do to earn me crust. No, don't you look down on me, even wiv me drinkin' and whorin' I was still a lady an' don't you forget it.

13

THREE

By spring his father was back, stoked by the fires of religious fervour into even more of a monster. His efforts to beat religion into him failed utterly, for he turned back on God and all organised religion. The scourge of the world he thought of it, the source of all evil. But then all such religions had at their heart hate and fear. School continued once again after the cold winter and nothing changed there for him He was viewed with suspicion by all the children who marked him down as different yet in a way they could not fathom. But the bullying stopped. The tide had turned, they were scared of him. His silence unsettled them. Unnerved them. So be it.

Then came a succession of moves as his father dragged them all the country in search of souls to save. Barren landscapes the length and breadth of the country in inhospitable towns with their run down schools and run down folk. After six long dreary years his father's love affair with spreading the word far and wide died when his wife died unexpectedly. In her sleep apparently, a good way to go they all said. Yes, there were the odd cries of foul play as there always is, but his father wasn't even in the house at the time, being busy preaching hellfire to the local peasant who lapped it up, that is when they were not laughing at him. No, just he and his mother in the house and he had not seen or heard anything untoward. Heart failure was the verdict although the bloodshot eyes remained a puzzle.

That's when he met his Uncle for the first time. George. Completely different to his brother. A man of the world to be sure. You can't keep the boy yourself you must know that, it's not fair to him. You can get on with your saving souls and the boy can come live with me. And that was how it happened. His meagre possessions packed into one bag he left the latest of his family homes. Not a word did he say to his father and nor did he give him a backward glance. He had *his* salvation now.

And it tasted good.

Twelve years old, a new family, a new start. Addington, far enough away from London to be accounted completely rural. Uncle George and Aunt Katherine had a set of rules that he was expected to follow, but there was no hardship involved; most of the time he was left to his own devices to wander at will through the woods and lanes of that part of Surrey. His cousin Emily was three years older and her place in the family hierarchy was well established. Polite to his face at formal occasions such as meal times and when visitors were received, but at all other times she maintained an icy silence and indifference towards him. His uncle and aunt thought her an angel, a delicate flower of a girl, almost too good to be true. Of course, it wasn't true. As he would find out. As they would find out.

It had been decided that school would begin again for him in September when he would be thirteen. Surrey County School, boy, he was told. The best education hereabouts that can be had, boy. But that was a while off yet and he had no need to worry himself about it for a while yet. Only two weeks had gone by; it was the longest time in his short life that he had gone without a beating. All he could do now was imagine the pain, the tears, the bare skin exposed in readiness...there was a visceral pleasure in this, almost a longing for the pain, for the exposure. There was an overwhelming desire to be the victim. It was only then he realised it. A shiny new sixpence given to him by his uncle, thrown in the river. I lost it, it must have fallen out of my pocket, he said. The sympathy shown to him was an enormous fillip; it made the manufactured pain of losing the money so much easier to bear. There would be no replacement, even his uncle was not that kindly, but that perversely just made him feel better. Victim, he was a victim. There was only one thing that could crown it, to find victims himself. He was no stranger to that however. Gaining trust came easily to him. Even in his own small sphere of experience. He was believed, he was an innocent. Seemingly. It gave him a power that others could only guess at. A leverage. To be used when necessary.

Surrey County School took away four years of his life, that's how it felt at the time, although he knew he was clever, he surprised himself with how he prospered academically. Gifted he was told. You will go far in your life boy. In biology he was the star pupil. Very committed, during break times he was often to be found partaking in some extra dissecting. Quiet, reserved in class was the oft made comment on various school reports. But then, there was that slight speech impediment that had travelled with him from childhood and speaking in class was just too painful for him. He would at once become red-faced and stammer in a pronounced way he never did normally. The laughs of his fellow schoolboys echoed in his ears and the name-calling became habitual, but there were ways of dealing with that. There would be a reckoning, a come-uppance or two coming someone's way. Best they said their prayers he thought. Sport, now that was something he hated with a passion at school. Not so much the sport itself although God knows that was dreary enough, but the ritual

16

humiliation of the communal showers, the communal laughs, the communal teasing. He was not built as the others, short legs, a protruding belly and that was not all. I feel sorry for your wife if you ever get one said Winters. What good would that be to her? Still, let me know and I might be able to help out, tiny Jim. Winters, being the perfect specimen of manhood had his cronies who perfected the ability to laugh and guffaw on Winter's cue. Even this example of unblemished, flawless youth was as prone as any other to the slings and arrows of life. His fall from grace came with the fall from his bicycle. How ungainly he looked as he toppled. Bee sting everyone said for they had seen his hand come up to his face moments before with a look of surprise and pain on his face. It was unfortunate that his fall coincided with the approach of the number 61 omnibus. Catapult skills never leave you it is said.

FOUR-TWO

I never did the like the name Eliza, but my pa had a liking for it and that was that. My ma never got much of a look in when it came to making decisions whatever they might be. At least they did the decent thing and got married when I came along; now that may just have been ma's doing so perhaps I was wrong about her not getting her own way. I was not an only child for long; three sisters came along at various intervals, the last of them when I was in my teens, but I have my own theory about that. No, I will not be tempted to share it with you thank you very much. I was nineteen when the final sibling poked his head into the world. Fountain they called him; pity the poor lad who has to grow up with a name like that. There I was, a skivvy to my mother, helping to raise this tribe. All the time I wanted to get out and make my own way in the world, well, who wouldn't? But those sisters and brother of mine just got in the way and you could say I resented them for it and if you did, you would be right. Not that any of them liked me anyway, not even Emily who at least was a similar age to me, not that stopped her being demanding. I was convinced that I was destined to be a spinster, not that I wanted to be, but meeting men, suitable for marriage or otherwise was not an easy thing to do with all the fetching, skivvying and chores I had to do week in, week out. John asked me twice before I eventually accepted, well, I was twenty-eight and I figured it was him or the shelf. He was a cousin on my ma's side, first or second I don't recall nor did I much care to be honest. Of course we couldn't afford a place of our own at first; well I guess you could say we never really had a place of our own. Mind you, the addresses we did live at sounded rather grand; Montpelier Place, Brook Mews, South Bruton Mews. South Bruton Mews, that was Berkeley Square you know, Mayfair you know. They might have sounded grand, but they weren't. The Mews houses were little more than stables, well, I guess that's what they were alright. John was a coachman you see, I think he loved his horses more than he loved me, all the time he took over fussing them and grooming them. He used to reckon that he could polish a horse's coat so fine that he could see his face in it, not that I ever saw the point in that. Soon, I had children of my own to feed and money got tighter and never stretched as far as it should have done. Well, we both liked the odd tipple and I reckon we deserved it too. I always hold that Windsor was our downfall. John reckoned that it was a great chance for us to get out of London and into the country. He painted a rosy picture alright, I'll give him that. Country walks, river walks, all kinds of blessed walks. I never did work out when he thought we would find the time for all this walking; he was working all the time and when he wasn't he was at the pub. I had more than enough on my plate what with our son John being born a cripple. I could not cope with anything like that and he had to be taken into a home for the infirm. He's still with us though; don't worry about that, even getting some schooling that other buggers are paying for. No sooner than all that happened than little Emily got a sickness, it was terrible to see her in pain and looking so bad. The doctor said straightaway it was meningitis and we both knew what that meant. Within a short while she was gone, rest her little soul. We still had our little Annie, but it wasn't enough for me, I can't think of any other way of putting it. It's fair to say and I want to be honest about it, that yes, I took to drink more and more. Not just me, but poor John as well and that didn't help with his job, no one wants a drunken coachman. Yes, I had a few encounters with the police in Windsor, well, I can't deny it, I guess there's a public record of it somewhere, and the police do like to write everything down don't they. I think that one report they made about me said I had 'drunken and immoral ways'. Charming, I thought, what do they know, just because I had a liking for the odd rum or two, they trample all over my good character with their hob-nail boots. I first met 'the pensioner' in Windsor you know, but I'll get to him in a minute, but he was a real gent. What with the drinking and everything me and John went our separate ways. He was a good sort really, I don't want to run him down too much, he was good to me I guess. Anyway, I got a ten-shilling postal order from him every week, well, not every week, but it was steady enough for me. I upped sticks and went back to the city. I reckoned that the ten shillings would help keep the wolf from the door and if I found myself a little job too then so much the better. Well, I did my best, I sold flowers and made antis, not that I made much money, but at least it was an honest living, not like what I was forced into later. Sivvy and me, we were quite an item until the money ran out. The postal orders just stopped and I thought now, now John what gives here, have you found yourself another woman to spend your money on? Not that I would blame him if he had. Then I just happened to meet his brother who told me John had died of the drink. I was very cut up about it and not just because of the money either. We had been man and wife and brought up children together, well, apart from crippled John of course. It was only natural to be upset, put me in mind of poor Emily. Anyway, that was how the money stopped and Sivvy ran out on me. I found myself a little corner of Stratford, the Bow end you know and I had a few clients there who were spilling to spend a few pennies on me. Don't treat me too harshly, I had to find money for lodgings, beds don't grow on trees you know. It's not as if I gave up the other work completely. My crochet work was still pretty fine if I say so myself and my antis were sought after. I had myself a regular bed at Crossingham's, always found the money for it

20

even if I left it a little late sometimes. All I wanted to do sometimes was sleep; my breathing was becoming worse and worse in spite of the medicine I took for it. Not long for this world Annie, I thought to myself. I was right there wasn't I?

FIVE

No one guessed and no one knew, but he was left alone, just as before. Although there were still scores to settle, but they could wait, he was in no particular hurry. He had a notion that doctoring was for him, yes there was hard work involved, but he was single-minded and knew that would be no great barrier. Besides, all his tutors praised his quick brain. James can turn his hand to anything they said. He can do whatever he wants in life. It was true then as it was later. Other boys were more gifted perhaps, but then he was not above copying their work after 'borrowing' it from their desks, although borrowing is not quite the word to use. They never saw their work again. He was suspected, but when various pieces of work were found in another boy's desk, that was that. In spite of protestations of innocence, young Carruthers was expelled. It was not just the act of cheating, but also found in his desk were examples of what the headmaster termed 'shameful and disgusting images and words'. Carruthers was no great loss to the school, the kind of boy who laughs at another's speech problems was not deserving of a fine and proper education.

He was always aware of this dark side to his character, but he did nothing to try and check it. Why should he, for it brought its own benefits and pleasure. And although he was supremely aware, others were not. Outwardly he was steadfastly normal with barely a ripple of contrariness disturbing his very ordinariness. His uncle and aunt saw nothing in him that they did not expect to see. How easy are people to fool. Take his uncle for instance.

22

A solicitor in London, with fine offices in High Holborn which reflected his professional success. The smell of the beeswax polish on his uncle's rich, mahogany desk was one of the clearest olfactory memories that James possessed. His uncle harboured great hopes that he would follow him into this formal, rigid world and he wasted no opportunity in dragging a reluctant James off to London for the day. While his uncle was invariably tied up with work, James would make his escape. Down Cock Lane to Smithfield market or up to Bart's where he wandered at will, always having a ready-made excuse for why he was there should he be challenged. Sometimes he would wallow in the quagmire and dregs of humanity to be found in St. Giles rookery. He would strike out for Whitechapel often, where life was just as grim and just as fascinating for him. But his uncle was not a fool for wanting or believing James had any interest whatsoever in the mundane world of soliciting and conveyancing. No, he was a fool because of what happened in the family home when he was absent.

James only came across the affair, yes, let's call in an affair, by chance. He was absent from school on account of contracting measles. Once the contagion had passed he still had two weeks of further quarantine to contend with. Sleeping fitfully one morning after consuming a hurriedly conceived and executed breakfast, served by Bessie who had the rest of the day off and was impatient to be gone, he heard noises, odd noises which emanated from the west wing of the house. Throwing a robe over his pyjamas he set off to investigate. To him, it sounded like souls in pain, like something out of Dante's Inferno. He couldn't have been further from the truth. His heart in his mouth, he stopped outside his aunt's room. This was where the sounds originated from. He thought about opening the door and marching in, but he, by this time, was well aware of what these noises signified. An eye to the keyhole confirmed these thoughts. There was his aunt, half naked, with Simeon Matthews, a friend of his uncle's, underneath her. Thrashing wildly on the bed with an intensity that almost frightened James, their animal howls filled the air, until the moment of their shared release, which coincided with his own release. He was immediately aware that it was not just witnessing the act itself which had aroused and excited him; it was knowing that it gave him a power he could exercise. An opportunity for exploitation that was now in his hands.

In the days before he returned to school, he was careful to let it be known that he was out ambling in the woods for the day or walking into Coulsdon, before returning to the house in the hopes of catching his aunt and her lover. He did not have long to wait. He saw from his window the figure coming up the drive. Confident, assured. But not Simeon Matthews. But a near-neighbour, Jacob Willoughby. A social call perhaps? A very social call as it turned out. The footsteps that came up the stairs sounded every bit as assured and confident as the man himself appeared to be.

When he heard the soft closing of the bedroom door, he crept along to his viewpoint. He was not to be disappointed. They were certainly not strangers to each other's bodies he thought as he watched their slow undressing, their excitement mirroring his own. The waves of pleasure which engulfed them also engulfed him and suddenly he realised all was quiet in the room and he felt sure they would hear his hard breathing, even through the stout, wooden door. He lay back on his own bed, drained.

But what was to be done about it. Tell his uncle, no…not yet. Confront his aunt, yes, but not it was not confronting he had in mind, but bargaining.

The voices began their infernal whispering a few short weeks ago. Snatches of sentences, even a song. Fragmentary and disjointed, but with a common aim. They came to him at all hours of the day and night. Best I say my prayers then. Best you say your prayers. And what was that? Violets I picked from my mother's grave. Murder, now it's murder. Murder. There is no way out, he can see that. He cannot flee from them, he cannot hide, cannot escape.

Please, no. He doesn't want to see them. Hearing their voices is torture enough. Seeing them would send him over the edge.

Yes, they chorus. The edge.

The edge of the abyss.

SIX-THREE

You English. Always you want to be the best at everything. You want your summers to be the warmest, even your winters to be the coldest. Call these winters cold? I could tell you a thing or two about winters. I was even born in the winter and Swedish winters, now they can be mind-numbingly cold. And a Swedish farm is about as bleak as it comes. But that was my lot, to be born to hard working God-fearing folk who looked on their farm as both bounty and blessing. It never seemed that way to me. I spent nearly all my waking moments in thoughts of how I would make my escape. And at sixteen, escape came. Endless rows with my parents had taken their toll on all of us. How can you not know your catechism, child? And just look at the dust on that bible of yours, living proof that you do not pick it up from one day to the next. As glad as I was to go and even now you cannot really believe how glad I was, I think they were more so to have me go. I had cousins in Carl Johan parish. Not that I had any intention of staying with them for long, not with the whole city at my feet. I was ill-fitted for anything other than domestic work which is where Lars comes in. I liked Lars from the start although his children were brats, all four of them. My cousin, Bengt introduced us and I agreed to help out Lars with the children and domestic duties. It was soon after that the whispers started and the gossip mongers got to work. *I heard that the young girl that Lars employs shares his bed as well as the house. Ya, I heard that too, such a scandal. Ah well, nothing to worry about there, Anna has been to see the pastor, he will put matters right.* So, the pastor comes around and sticks his nose into our business. Now, let me tell you something about pastors, they are holier than thou

26

hypocrites. It was a pastor who ran off with Lar's wife and they seem to think they have the God-given right to lecture us about our lives. We ran him out the house between us and laughed about it all evening. Lars had more to laugh about than most, a young girl to share his bed, to cook his meals and feed his children. We laughed together that night, but it wasn't long before he laughed alone. Then, one day I had been at the local meat market buying up scrag ends with the little money I had been given and when I arrived home laden down like a donkey, I found Beata, Lar's wife there. Instead of throwing her out, Lars greeted her with open arms. Suddenly, I found myself sleeping in the small, cold room at the back of the scullery and my work load doubled. My food was rationed and my already pitiful allowance was cut back to almost nothing. *You have a bed, Elisabet, you are fed, what more do you want? Are we not good to you? Think yourself lucky to have a roof over your head. Other girls of your age find themselves on the streets.* Yes, Beata, thank you, Beata. How grateful I am, Beata. That woman drove me crazy. And Lars stood by and did nothing. Except he still made approaches to me, but I vowed never again. And I kept that vow. When I heard of another family in need of help I offered my services, they were in the Cathedral parish and had not heard the rumours about my morals or looseness. They were glad to have me, but God, the work was so hard and the family so dull that I was soon tired of them and their ways. *Other girls of your age find themselves on the streets.* It probably would have pleased Beata very much to find out how right she was. I was young still, pretty and no so worn out that I could not show certain gentlemen a good time, provided they paid the right price. Lars might have had it for nothing but by God I would make sure the others paid in hard cash. Then, I found myself with child. I was determined to keep the baby no matter what. Yes, I knew it would be hard. And as for the father, well how could I possibly know who was the father? Whoever it was I would not have wanted their help not that they would have offered any aid anyway. It was not to be, my little girl was still-born. Motherhood was never to beckon again. As for the pennies, well they kept rolling in. I was not much bothered by the police unless I strayed out my area. I was registered with them which meant I was free to work in peace, but also meant I had to be carted off to the hospital often for examinations. Disease was always around and I contracted a chancre in the same year I lost my daughter. After a few degrading trips I was told I was clean and given a lecture on my way of life. I had heard it all before. They did not tell me where to find a proper job. Not that I wanted one. What? You are shocked? You English, so quick to see the good in people and so quick to be shocked at other's sins which could not possibly be your own. Tch. The English, it's odd that I think of that now, it was thanks to you English that I got out of Sweden. Well, one Englishman in particular who was always very kind to me when we met. I can't tell you who he was or what he did, very secret he told me that his line of work was, but he asked me to come back to London with him. I never really knew what he had in mind for me as I ran off as soon as we arrived at his house. Near Hyde Park it was. I knew roughly where the Swedish parish was and made my way there throwing myself on their mercy with tales of beatings and worse aboard ship and how I feared for my life. I think, secretly, it was just the kind of thing they loved hearing. Made them feel better and oh so superior to see how low their countrymen or women could fall. I could be full of sob stories when I needed them and I always seemed to need them. Anyway, here I was in London and now what I thought? Men would have always of need of me and London was not so full of whores that I couldn't earn a bit for myself. Now, don't get completely the wrong idea about me, it wasn't all whoring, if I could earn an honest penny or two, I would. I met Johnny that way, through flower selling. He was in drink and stumbled against me, knocking my flower basket to the

28

ground. He was a real gent, paid for all the ruined flowers. We began to see a bit of each other. Yes, you are right, he was older than me, but I had known a lot of older men and I had no complaints to offer against any of them except that bastard, Lars. Now you recall me mentioning an honest living, of course you do. Here is honest for you, me and Johnny set ourselves up with a nice little coffee shop. Down in Poplar it was. This was after we was wed. Me, a wife? About time I thought. The trouble with me and Johnny was that we spent too much of our time together, working, eating and sleeping. I don't know about you, but I don't think it healthy for a couple, don't seem natural to me. But you probably have your own ideas about that. It was hard work mind, long hours and every time the rent went up we just fund somewhere else to go to then start all over again. He was never any kind of businessman was Johnny and I did the best I could, in the only way I knew how, to get some extra shillings. If you had asked him he would have said he didn't know anything about my 'extra work' and if he had known he would have put a stop to it. And that would have been nonsense; he knew about it alright, you might even call him a pimp although he would have been as useless as that as running a coffee shop. Typical man; let the women do all the work for them and live off the proceeds. Had him pegged though. When a customer made us an offer for the coffee shop, we gladly let it go and good luck to the fellow. John Dale was his name, an ugly man who had the manners of a pig and the charm of a carthorse. Don't know how he did with it, never went back to Poplar, not until nearly the end anyway. We rented a hovel off Brick Lane. In a dirty, rat-infested and overcrowded alley. Neighbours who would just as soon kill you as be forced to talk to you. Neighbourliness, there's a joke. I did a bit of charring and sewing to make ends meet. My eyes were good and my needlework was very fine if I say so myself when I could keep my hands still. The drink had taken its hold on me and I gave in to it. It gave me a release from the sheer boredom of everyday life. Yes, I know it sounds shallow, but you weren't there in my boots so don't tell me yes you know how it was. It won't wash with me. Do you think I liked being in the workhouse? And Whitechapel workhouse at that? No, you know nothing about it so stop judging me or pitying me, which is even worse.

SEVEN-ACT ONE

PONDICHERRY LODGE, ADDINGTON

INTERIOR PARLOUR. IT IS MORNING

AK: *What? You are saying what to me?*

JD: *You heard me perfectly well, Aunt Katherine. I have no need to repeat myself.*

AK: *And what do you intend to do with this knowledge that you gained by spying on me young man? Do you intend to lay all this before my husband as your religious maniac of a father would have done? Do you want to shame me?*

JD: *You have my proposal.*

AK: *Your proposal horrifies me.*

JD: *As to that, your behaviour horrifies me but not to the extent it should hence my proposal.*

AK: *And you really think I am going to take a boy like you into my bed? You are crazier than I thought. My lovers and I do not deny I have them, after all you have seen them through my keyhole you disgusting boy, are generous gentlemen, they give me gifts, trinkets and what can you give me besides the obvious? And I am not convinced you can even provide that.*

JD STANDS UP WALKS OVER TO HIS AUNT'S CHAIR, BRINGS HIS FACE TO HERS.

JD: *I can reward you with silence. That is the gift I bring to your bed.*

AK SLAPS HIS FACE AND PACES THE ROOM. SHE FINALLY SETTLES BACK DOWN.

AK: *And if I were to call your bluff?*

JD: *My dear aunt Katherine, look at me and then decide. And pray you make the right decision.*

AK: *I am not accustomed to being bullied by sixteen year old boys in my own home. Perhaps I will confess all to my husband and throw myself on his mercy or stand my ground and deny any wrongdoing. You may find yourself branded a liar and the villain of the piece.*

JD: *That, of course, is up to you and your own conscience. But armed with dates, times and names I am sure my beloved uncle will arrive at his own conclusion.*

AK: *Is this how you repay us for taking you in? You are a bastard of the highest order which is sad for one so young.*

JD: (UNDER HIS BREATH) *And you, madam, are a whore of the highest order.*

JD: *I will await your answer shortly. You will find me in the drawing room.*

AK: *You sicken and disgust me.*

JD: *So it would appear. A very moral viewpoint from someone who thinks nothing of taking lovers to the detriment of her marriage and the betrayal of her husband.*

AK: *And what of your own morals? I cannot see that I would ever stoop as low as you. You bemoan my betrayal as you call it of my husband yet you seem to have no difficulty in wanting to bed me yourself. If I am the sinner you make me out to be then you are doubly so.*

JD: *You are quite right. Guilty on all counts. I will leave you to your thoughts and guilt.*

JD EXITS AND AK SLUMPS IN CHAIR, HEAD IN HANDS.

SEVEN-ACT TWO

PONDICHERRY LODGE, ADDINGTON

EVENING. INTERIOR. AN UPSTAIRS BEDROOM

AK: *So much for that. And what was that?* SHE LAUGHS LOUDLY ALMOST HYSTERICALLY.

JD: SCREAMING *Stop that. Stop!*

AK: *Not so much of the big man now are we? Hah and I mean that in every way. You pathetic little boy. Go ahead if you like, tell my husband whatever you like and I will have some choice things to say too. I think we are done here now, don't you? Get out!*

JD LOOKS AS THOUGH HE IS ABOUT TO SAY SOMETHING BUT APPEARS TO CHANGE HIS MIND

AK: *Are you deaf as well? Get out!*

JD EXITS STAGE LEFT PURSUED BY EMBARRASSMENT HUMILIATION AND PAIN. AND A COLD HEART BENT ON REVENGE.

WHORE. WHORE.

EIGHT

He was shamed, but not ashamed. Humiliated, but not down. His aunt's behaviour and lax ways did not change; he had not expected that it would. But for the most part he was back in school away from her knowing looks. Still, he knew the pattern of her lover's comings and goings and it was a simple matter to send an anonymous letter, written by a fellow pupil who knew only too well that the threat of violence made against him was no idle threat, to his uncle advising him to come back home on a certain date at a certain time. He derived a certain amount of pleasure in picturing his uncle walking in on his wife while she was being pleasured by one of the local gentry. Of course, he could scarcely have foreseen the horrific results of his actions he reasoned to himself. The inquest and subsequent investigation did not discover whether his aunt fell to her death from the window accidentally or deliberately. There was a strong suspicion that his uncle had perhaps helped her on her way to eternity, but there was no evidence to suggest such a thing. The erstwhile lover was not a witness to the events, having been preoccupied with dressing whilst running down the stairs. An open verdict was returned. The matter of the anonymous accusing letter was all but forgotten. His uncle was to remain a broken man for the rest of his days. Betrayed by his wife, forsaken by his own daughter whose marriage to a handsome Hussar officer was her passport to another life and scorned by his nephew.

He set about contacting local dealers and selling off family heirlooms. The money he thought was rightfully his, he was family after all. If he could have sold the house out from underneath his uncle than he would have done so, but at sixteen there were still some things beyond him as a minor. His uncle hardly noticed the disappearance of silver, books and furniture. He was haunted by his wife's infidelity and her final moments. *I don't know how she attracted so many lovers, Uncle. Eh? What's that, James? I was just saying that Aunt Katherine was not the most skilful lover, I found her charmless.* His parting shot. That should give him something to think about.

Now. What to do now? Where to go? Not back to school that was for sure. He knew no one outside of school and family And family meant nothing to him, not that there was any family left that he was aware of. Emily had married her soldier boy and they had made their home in Chelsea near the barracks. He could go there as a temporary measure, not that he would be made particularly welcome. His relationship with Emily had never improved. They distrusted each other, found fault with each other. And the dashing Captain Truscott was a crashing, monumental bore whose twin topics of conversation were sport and soldiering. He had no idea why Emily would have wished to tie herself to this crashing bore of a man.

Needs must as they say. And so he found himself on their doorstep one morning. With tales of Emily's father's drunken rages and unprovoked assaults on the boy. He knew he would be believed, he always was and the self-inflicted bruises and cuts he displayed to them helped to make his case even more convincing. You can't stay here long was their mantra; this place is scarcely big enough for the two of us they said. I'll help around the house he said dutifully, fetch and carry. Not that he had any intention of doing so. But as a means to an end it worked, for London was now his base, his home, his city. A butcher's in Fulham Broadway needed an assistant, yes, the work was beneath him, but he took it for the money and the sheer joy and exuberance he felt when carving, slicing and cleaving. No artist could have been more enamoured of their brushwork than he was with his butchery skills. The knives became part of him, like an extension of his own arm, cutting through the flesh. And the very smell of the carcasses and the blood, it gave him a pleasure that he had never known before. To the horror of his cousin he would arrive home covered in blood. She may have guessed that he slept in his bloodied apron; if she did she said nothing.

When he was not working, he paced the streets, covering miles and miles of the city, taking in the sights and sounds, living and breathing them. The city lived for him as an entity of its own; it had an extraordinary heartbeat of love, regret and lives both futile and satisfied. A city which sold itself to all and sundry like a common whore and enticed lovers anew with promises and riches. A city which had no need of sleep for it was continually refreshing itself, re-inventing itself almost, appearing to be all things to all people. Within its walls you could find fortune, you could find wealth or an early grave. The city gave life and snatched it away when you least expected it. He was mesmerised by it, but he was young and the city had yet to deal him the harsh blows it would.

His first lesson would be the simplest of all; don't get caught. Simple, but for some so difficult to put into practice. And with so many things, he learnt the hard way. Next door to the butcher's there was a laundry. The businesses shared a common yard. He was often to be found sharing time with some of the laundry employees and occasionally being invited into their canteen. Canteen they called it, but it was one very small room, no bigger than a cloakroom, which seemed to be its chief purpose. He spoke little, but he listened, oh how he listened to them prattle on about their sad little lives. There were nuggets of gold amongst the conversational dross. *I'll tell you people, I don't trust no bank, I keeps all of my money under the bed. What money is that Fred; you piss it all up the wall down the pub each night? I've got some put by, don't you worry about that. You're lucky Fred, I spend what I earn, and look here's last week's wages in my pocket. I like to keep my money with me at all times.* Which pub do you drink in, Fred? Oh yes I know it. We must have a drink together one night. It's a fair step from my place mind; still, if I have too much to drink I could always kip at yours eh? These people were so easy, so very easy. He was careless though. A wallet in a coat pocket. A pilfering of a pound note. Daylight, a crowded laundry. He was seen. The Magistrates Court was unduly lenient, he had a story to soften their hearts, that came easily to him too. Still, he had to serve two weeks in prison and his employment at the butcher's was at an end. On his release he walked to Emily's, a long enough walk for one weakened by incarceration. Emily and the dashing Captain knew well enough his release date, for his meagre possessions were stacked neatly by the door. Not the stoutest of doors. And Emily's dresses were not made from the strongest material for his knife cut through them like butter. For many years Emily would recount this story and think herself extremely fortunate not to be home that day.

And now he had to start again. There was a widow woman, Mary who was employed by the laundry. She lived in Hammersmith and had a soft spot for him. Even after his fall from grace she may still have that same soft spot and if she did he would cultivate it. No one ever doubted his charm and few were immune from it. He knew where she lived for he had spent one or two interminable evenings with her, listening to tales of her departed husband. If this was her idea of courting God help her. Mary, hullo. Hullo James. A cold reception, but she thawed my how she thawed. Feet under the table and in her bed, not that she expected much there and he certainly had no desire for her. His perfunctory attempts at love-making seemed to satisfy her. Perhaps, at thirty-eight she had lost all such desires herself. The basement room she occupied in Beryl Road was cramped, dingy and had long ago given up any pretensions to being a proper home and he vowed to get out as soon as he could. From the steps he could almost throw a stone into the grounds of Fulham hospital and while waiting for gainful employment he stalked its corridors. A white coat was easy to come by and with all these things it was a matter of confidence, he walked the corridors of the hospital as if he belonged there and in spite of his youth he was never challenged, Always look and act the part, another lesson. The pickings were rich, in the course of a single week he made over £12 from careless doctors, nurses and patients alike. Careful not to overplay his hand he retired from the 'medical profession' after three weeks of pilfering and mischief. Don't get caught, you see, he had learned.

NINE-FOUR

We are made of strong stuff, us from the Black Country. The whole family walked to London, can you believe it? All the way from Wolverhampton bless us. I was six years old and thought it a real adventure. My dad was a tin worker, a good tin worker too, but he had no choice but to down tools when there was a strike in 1848. He had no idea when the strike would end or what jobs would be left at the end of it so that was it, he had a family to feed so off we went to London. Dad found work in the at Bermondsey leather market, lord what a stench there was there, and mum took in washing. Dear old mum pegged out when I was thirteen; I think she was just worn out with life. I was lucky I suppose because I was allowed to continue my education at St John's Charity School, but my younger sisters and brothers were carted off to Bermondsey Workhouse. I lived with my dad for a while, but then he ups and dies too and up pops an aunt who decides that Wolverhampton is the best place for me. At thirteen I was in no position to argue. Bison Street was not a bad place to be any road and Dowgate School was a happy kind of school where everyone got along. I wouldn't say my schooling was very good, but I was educated enough to get by in the world. Mr and Mrs Knowles who lived next door to my aunt were a kindly couple who had lived in their Bison Street home for over fifty years. She was always baking from morning till night, enough to feed the five thousand. They were both skinny as rakes so Lord knows where they put it all. I had the first pick of the loaves and the cakes that came out of Mrs Knowles's old-fashioned oven. I cannot think of her without smelling yeast and flour. Granny Knowles I called her, I remember thinking, perhaps she was born old. I've lost my thread now, where was I? Oh yes, the Knowles's had a grandson who would occasionally pay them a visit. Thomas Conway he was. Tom. A soldier, although he had just left the Royal Irish. A fine man with words he was. He would write me poems, lovely little things they were, what a clever man he was. He set himself up as a writer of people's lives, local people mostly who were usually notorious in one way or another. We travelled all over; Birmingham, Dudley, Walsall, Sutton Coldfield, Coventry, Nuneaton and made a penny or two. Public hangings were a godsend to us. We would get as much information we could about those who were for the drop and if we failed we would invent something. These gallows ballads were very popular and we were in demand. Making a living from other's misery I suppose you could say, but that's how man operates isn't it? I got my chance to write my own words instead of leaving it to Tom when it was my cousin who was about to hang. A crowd of over a thousand turned up to see Christopher Robinson cut off, nasty brutish man who was always going to up end up on the scaffold in my opinion. No loss there. By then I had been delivered of a darling little girl, Annie who my aunt looked after when we were on the road selling our little books. My aunt was determined to see me and Tom wed, but we were having none of that. A blessing and a bit of paper meant nothing did it? We were happy as we were, for a while at least. After the two boys came along I wanted to settle down, but Tom was too much of a traveller to give up that part of his life so we struggled on. When Annie was sixteen it all became too much for me and we split for good and I took Annie with me back to London and left the boys with Tommy. My sister Eliza got us into Cooney's a reputable lodging house. I loved Flower and Dean Street in spite of the poverty and squalor; it had a real heart to it even if it didn't have a Granny Knowles! That's where I met my John. Such a sweet lovely man, he sold fruit at the market so we never went hungry. Annie got herself a job at a milliners on Tower

41

Green which is where she met young Louis who was a reporter, a proper writer. Before you could say Jack Robinson she had got herself hitched and headed off to Bermondsey. To make extra money we went hop picking in Kent every year me and John. Back breaking work, but we made money and made friends every time we went. The local people resented us for taking work away from them, but I'll tell you what, I never saw any of them queuing to take our places. No matter how many times we scrubbed ourselves we always smelt of hops, it got into your skin somehow and stayed there. We ignored the special trains laid on for hoppers and walked there and back. Made of strong stuff us Black Country folk, told you that didn't I?

TEN-SOUNDS

Oi! Mind where you are going with that barrow, boy, nearly had me bleedin' foot off. Sorry, guv. Don't guv me just watch it. Leave the boy alone Billy. Here's another of them organ-grinders, Gawd knows how any of you lads make any money, can't cross the road without falling over one of you. Try Bethnal Green, heard they like music down that way. You with the basket, sling it over here, almost given up waitin' for you I had. Looking to do some business darling? I'll see you right. Hold up, cabbie; look out mate, your fare's trying to do a runner. Nah, mate not me unless you're going to show me the colour of your money, go after him yourself. Hot muffins here, come and get them. Here, this is my patch go and sell your hokey-pokey elsewhere, bugger off. Hokey-pokey freshly made, only a halfpenny, didn't you hear him eytie, bugger off, no one wants your hokey bleedin' pokey here. Don't know why they can't stick to Saffron Hill where they belong. Hear, hear mate. Any scissors to grind? Any knives to sharpen? A quick guaranteed service. Flowers! Pretty bunches, picked this morning. What about you, sir? A bunch for the little lady waiting patiently at home? You picked the right customer there love, old Sam has three women, none of them little and none of them ladies. Go on Sam, get your money out! Where you taking your fare then? Plaistow eh! Want to take my geezer with you? Nah, nothing like that, I just can't be bovvered. Thanks pal. Get your filthy hands off me! Oh, murder! There she goes again, put a sock in it love we've heard it all before. Blimey, what does a man have to do to get some rest around here?

43

ELEVEN-SOUNDS

Organs pumped.

Recorders blown.

Iron wheels on roads.

Horses trotting, steaming.

Shouts everywhere.

Buy this, buy that.

Balladeers singing.

Steam trains hissing.

Papers boys shouting the news.

Clashers of cymbals,

Beaters of drums.

Drunks singing.

Shouting

Howling.

Yelling.

Cursing.

Fighting.

Cabs hailed.

44

TWELVE-FIVE

Whatever I say you will accuse me of making it up so why should I bother? But perhaps I want to put the record straight while I can. Most of it you have got from Joe who got it from me so you know it's the bee's knees. First of all, there was no child ever, I have never been with child, I don't know why people want to make things up about me and even if had been a mother, what does it matter? I am only famous for one thing of course. I was born in Ireland; some people have got that right. Limerick, actually if you want the truth of it. I know what you lot say; you don't sound Irish. Nor would you if you only lived there for a year. My old man hankered after living in Wales, I don't know why and he is not around to ask. He earned enough in the iron industry to clothe and feed us all and I suppose we must be grateful for that. Sixteen and wed. No, not a childhood sweetheart. A steady man was William, a miner and a straight talker. If you ask me was it love, I don't know. The fact is that we wed and that's all you need to know. And when he got himself blown to bits I moved to Cardiff and lodged with a cousin. And to be blunt with you that's where I got my start in prostitution. I was like hundreds, maybe thousands of others who saw it simply as a means to an end. I had a terrible illness there and thought my time had come. Eight long months I lay in hospital. My cousin was glad to get shot of me; I had not been exactly helping with the income had I? I gathered what money I could and made my way to London. The nuns kept a place running for the likes of me in Providence Row and they must have been taken with me for instead of chucking me out the first chance they got they put me to work there, scrubbing floors and the like. After a week of two of that they found me a position in a large grocery shop in Cleveland Street. Just down the street from the workhouse it was, perhaps it was the nun's warning. Be a good girl or else. In comes one day a foreign lady, French she was and I straight away knew her for what she was, a working girl, dressed up to the nines maybe, but a working girl all the same. She took a shine to me straight off. Come and work for me, Mary she says one day, knowing I would know exactly what she meant. She had a house, a big house it seemed to me, near Hyde Park. I was given an allowance to go out and spend on new dresses and petticoats. And the biggest surprise to me was that she trusted me with the money. The clients were gentlemen, clean and generous. I earned more in a week than I would in three months at the shop. And I was fed, clothed and not worked too hard. I felt like a proper lady. And then, wonders of wonders, one of my regulars, a Frenchman proposed to take me to Paris. He was granted permission to do so by Madame M. It sounded grand, me in Paris, riding in carriages up and down this boulevard and that boulevard, but I soon grew tired of that life and wanted to come home. Homesick for London, I must have been mad. I was suddenly out of favour when I arrived back in London and life became that much harder. I told Madame M. exactly what I thought of the changes that had been made and was escorted to the door for my trouble. Slammed in my face it was. I trudged wearily across the city looking for a lodging house that I could afford with the few pennies in my purse. Tossed from pillar to post until I came to the Ratcliffe Highway. Was directed to a small house in St. Georges Street where I found an odd woman who went by the name of Mrs. Buki. I told her my story with a few added extra pieces thrown in for sympathy. She was a good woman to work for, as long as I did as I was told and serviced the clients enthusiastically I was pretty much free to do as I pleased. She even took me to

46

Madame M's and demanded that my dresses be returned to me. Not that it got us anywhere; we were strong-armed away from the door by two of Madame's 'helpers' who advised us that our health may be in danger if we tried to repeat our actions. Stuck up French cow. My drinking started to get out of hand shortly after that and I found myself back out on the streets, No, I don't blame anyone else, My liking for drink was to undo me many more times. Mrs Carthy's was my next stopping off point on my journey. Breezer's Hill, not much to say about it really. I paid for my bed. I slept in it. I went to work. Too many Joes. Joe in Stepney, the builder, Joe the mason in Bethnal Green. Both seemed to be fond of me, I mean they cared for me, but neither one could put up with me when I had drink inside me. Cooley's Lodging House, now that was a rum old place to live. You needed your wits about you if you wanted to steer clear of trouble. Keep your head down gal I told myself. Do what you have to do and leave it at that. Then, the third Joe appears out of the blue. Starts chatting to me in the middle of Commercial Street. Well, I thought, I know what you are after, but I was wrong there wasn't I? By the next day we had agreed to live together, just like that. He did a spot of portering at Billingsgate and some general labouring. He was a great drinker on occasion, but was put out by the fact that I could out-drink him and be on my feet when he was horizontal. He took it in good part though. We moved around a little, forced to really, landlords took exception to the fact we could not pay our rent and we were kicked out regularly until we settled at Millers Court. Wish to God I had never set eyes on the place.

THIRTEEN

He couldn't rely on pilfering alone. Somewhere within him, his own peculiar moral code told him that was somehow not right, although he was not averse to the notion of stealing to add to his wages. He drifted away from Mary, it was time to move on, about time he started making something of himself, started to make a name for himself. He always thought he would become somebody, someone who people took notice of. Ironic then, that his deeds would live on, but his name would remain unknown. He took his leave of Mary and also a few pounds of her savings. He almost felt guilty, but he had himself to consider and he had never showed compassion to the smallest of creatures, let alone those who professed to be close to him. Compassion was a weakness to be despised, a waste of precious time and energy. He was still young, he still had such a long way to, so why did he feel as though journey's end was unattainable, that the life he desired and he felt, deserved was out of reach and would remain so? He had guile and cunning. He had confidence, charm and a glib tongue, but already he could only see menial work as being his lot and that rankled. It was beneath him, he was ill-fitted for it. It was one thing knowing it, it was quite another to enable others to see it. In the meantime, he had immediate need of lodgings and employment. Gravitating towards the East End if for no other reason than he considered it to be the beating heart of the city, he took a position with Willets slaughterhouse who were in urgent need of a slaughter man, a job he took to readily and soon proved his worth in spite of his comparative youth.

Mile End Road was another world for him, both desolate and exciting, drab, but colourful. Coming alive at night in a way it never could by day, it was teeming with life. Narrow streets radiated from the main thoroughfares, like an almighty spider's web. Shop fronts barely illuminated by candlelight suddenly revealed a wizened old man or woman selling their wares. Small courts stand back from these streets, overflowing with families who spill out into steps, doorways and alleyways. Children were everywhere; impossible to say who they belonged to. He thought them almost feral; the intensity of their stares almost unnerved him. Large groups, although impossible in the impenetrable gloom to tell how large, gathered on street corners. To do what? he thought. Gossip, plan? Pipes are passed around and the smoke curls above their heads, lost to the fog. Here and there he can hear the sound of scuffles and fist-fights. Running feet fleeing the scene. Shouts of bravado which speak of revenge are lost on the night air as public houses swallow them up. The pubs themselves are great splashes of light amongst the blackness. Was this where he belonged, with this slice of humanity who refused to be bowed or beaten by their lowly station?

Certainly for now he did. A room in Stepney Green was his home. The building was owned by an astute Jew (were there any other kind he thought?) who had managed to cram twenty-eight people into the seven rooms he let out. Sleep was almost a luxury, there was never a stillness to the house, silence was unknown. He took to walking the streets at night; did nobody ever sleep? Even at 3am people filled the streets, some in search of pleasure some in search of drink (and they didn't have far to look) some going about their business. And whores, so many whores plying their 'wares'. Young, old, wretches of all ages, shapes and ability. For the most part drunk, degenerate and diseased. But, for all that, there were the occasional visits when the need became too strong to resist. *Never mind dear, I've seen all sorts in here, I don't suppose it will take long. Poor man, we all have our crosses to bear, I could tell you all kinds of tales. Hardly seems fair to take your money darling.* Each time he would tell himself it was worth the ritual humiliation, tell himself he was still young.

All his demons were now in place, some however lying dormant. Not that he thought of his own singular character traits as demons, he was not much given to introspection except when he felt wronged and then the soul-searching began in earnest, but then so did the methods whereby he could gain revenge.

For all the academic qualities he and others believed he possessed, he had nothing to show for it. His aunt, the whore, was to blame. He laid all his troubles at her door; at least she got what she deserved. He wasted no time in sympathy on those who were not worthy of it. The whole chain of events that led to her death was of her making, the lovers, the betrayal of her husband and her humiliation of him. Her choice, her decision. And now where was he? Earning a pittance in a slaughterhouse, paying a shilling a week for a hovel in Stepney Green. He did have skills that could not be denied. His knife work was superb, clean and quick and surprisingly skilful. But of what real use was that? Did he crave a life of slaughtering and butchering? Was that the sum total of his aspirations?

FOURTEEN-ONE

4d a night at Willoughby's, not bad I thought an' I know I can earn that easily like. Thrawl Street wasn't so bad either, it wasn't the worst street around and wasn't the best, just normal like. There were four of us sharin' the room an' we got on alright, we was good company for each other an' if one of us was short of doss money the others would 'elp out. Emily, now she was a nice old stick an' did more than the others an' me to keep things tidy like in our room. Anyway, you would 'ave found me in the Frying Pan that night, always good for a spot of business an' the landlord looked out for us gals. I was in the money that day alright, 'ad turned a few tricks an' got my doss money three times over, but bleedin' well spent it three time over too. Tried my luck anyway back at Willoughby's, but the deputy caught me in the kitchen wivout me money and slung me out into that filthy night. Lawd, how it thundered that night, never seen so many flashes of lightnin' before, must 'ave jumped a 'undred times or more. Still, told 'im I'd be back with me money before long. Pointed at a pretty bonnet I 'ad found. What do you think of me fine bonnet? It's only fine if it 'elps you get your doss, Polly 'e says. Like I always said, no good asking men 'bout things like that, they aven't a clue. Then I seen 'Em down on the corner of Osborn Street. She 'ad to give me an 'and as I nearly fell, well, I 'ad been drinkin' my doss money away and was well gone. Are you coming back, Polly? Soon I says, if not I know a place to stay, old 'Enry won't throw me out. Didn't get that far did I? I thought there's a nice looking gent. Fancy doing a bit of business, darlin'? 'Allo I

51

thought, got a quiet one 'ere. It's usually 4d love but you can 'ave me for 3d I says to him, how 'bout a 3d upright? 'E mumbled somethin', might 'ave been a yes, could 'ave been anything. Point was 'e seemed willin' enough. He steadied me as like I said, I was a bit under the drink, seemed a right gent unlike others I 'ad come across. Steady girl 'e says. We'll go in 'ere shall we? Whatever you say sir, I says to 'im all posh like. The rain had started to come down 'eavy like again an' I was 'oping for a bit of shelter while we did our business. This way 'e says. Lawd, what a voice 'e had, all soft like. 'E put his cloak over me and just then there was a huge flash and I could see by the sign I was in Buck's Row. He leaned in close like and there was another great flash of lightning and I could see 'is face clearly An evil face. A familiar face too, but I 'ad no time to think 'bout that. 'Ow did I ever mistake 'im for a gentleman? I looked into 'is eyes and prayed it would be quick.

It was.

DETRITUS

Black Straw bonnet trimmed with black velvet.

Reddish brown ulster with seven large brass buttons bearing the pattern of a woman on horseback accompanied by a man.

Brown linsey frock.

White flannel chest cloth.

Black ribbed wool stockings.

Two petticoats, one gray wool, one flannel. Both stenciled on bands "Lambeth Workhouse".

Brown stays (short).

Flannel drawers.

Men's elastic (spring) sided boots with the uppers cut and steel tips on the heels.

Possessions:

Comb.

White pocket handkerchief.

Broken piece of mirror (a prized possession in a lodging house).

The voices startle him with their clarity. They surround him on all sides. Sometimes in unison, sometimes individual voices raise themselves over the clamour. They will surely drag him down into the depths of madness he already knows that it is too late that point has been reached. All he needs now is to know what they need, what they want from him.

The edge. The abyss.

That's their goal, their aim.

He stumbles on into the dark night.

Pursued.

Hounded.

Hunted.

FIFTEEN

Liverpool. A gateway to the world. To the New World.
Now twenty-five years old. Still waiting to make his mark, but if a
man can make his mark anywhere then it would be in America.
Opportunities for all. London had lost its appeal for him; one job
had followed another in abbatoirs, butchers, dockyards, tanning.
None of them rewarding, none of them fulfilling. Liverpool was
the big stepping off point to the rest of the world and his future,
but instead became just another dead end. All he found in
Liverpool was more misery, squalor, violence, degradation and a
wife.

He came to the city with a little money; you could
describe it as a nest egg although he had formulated no real plans
to build any kind of nest. His thought, his only thought was to get
out, to clear out from these isles for good. Leave behind all those
who had hampered him in this so called life of his. There were so
many who had wronged him, so many he could blame for his
abject failure to amount to something; his parents, his uncle, his
cousin, his whoring aunt. They had all played their part in stunting
his growth. They all suffered for it too. It's no earthly use being a
victim unless you can hit back. Hurt those who hurt you was his
motto.

But yes, a wife. A nurse she was, Florence too of all
names a nurse could have. When they met he was certainly more
in need of a nurse than a wife. Liverpool was a rough city with
almost as many gangs as there were proper jobs to go around.

55

Everyone seemed to belong to one and the city was split between victims and those who made them so. Gangs for every street, all of them perfectly willing to defend their territory with whatever weapons came to hand. Catholics and Protestants had their own particular gangs who used religion as an excuse to beat and maim. For some reason that he could not fathom, the Catholic gangs were far more violent than their Protestant counterparts. Perhaps he thought it was the element of fear in their religion that resulted in this wholesale violence on their part; the Roach Guards and the Dead Rabbits were two of the nastiest who operated in the city and he counted himself fortunate not to have crossed their path. He was not so fortunate with the Cornermen. There may not have been a pub on every street corner in Liverpool but it certainly appeared that way and the Cornermen made their mark by loitering outside these pubs and intimidating passers-by into coughing up the price of a pint or more if they looked as though they had money to spare. If these toughs met with a refusal than the very least anyone could expect was a beating for their non-cooperation. Stabbings were not uncommon. He refused their unusual request. There were five of them outside this particular public house, armed with cudgels and sticks which they produced from under their coats. He was scared, he would admit to that, his stammer returned as he pleaded with them as the blows rained down. His eyes were drawn to the apparent ring-leader. I'll remember you he thought as his world went black.

It was two days he was told before he came round in the infirmary. The pain from his physical injuries was bad enough, but the hurt to his pride was huge. He hated not being in control and although he had often played the victim for his own ends he was unaccustomed to being in the position he now found himself in. His bloodied coat was slung over a chair next to the bed. With a monumental effort he managed to reach for it in spite of the pain that resulted. The money that he had oh so carefully saved, although stolen is perhaps a more apt word, and oh so carefully sewn into his coat was no longer there. He had not really expected it to be there to be honest. Penniless, beaten to a pulp and in a strange city; the world owed him. It really owed him.

She was just a shadowy figure at first. Formless even. As were all the staff he saw, whether doctors, nurses or cleaners. He could smell her above the carbolic, knew when it was her. His vision would improve one doctor told him, the swelling on his forehead would subside and when that happened he would be well on the road to recovery. A full recovery he asked through parched lips. Let's see shall we? One step at a time. Let's not walk before we can run. Time is a great healer. God, why can't doctors talk properly he thought? He had no need of their platitudes, just their ability to get him fit once more. That's all he wanted. Nurse Evans she announced to him. She talked to him like an adult not some errant uncomprehending child. She was gentle unlike some others whose ideas of how to bed bath someone they must have learned from the Marquis de Sade. But no, she was gentle. He had not known it from the start, but he was destined to have the hospital bed as a home for over a month, five weeks to be exact. Five long weeks, illuminated by Florence's presence only. Florence she had said, call me Florence. Thirty-five years old, a widow. Living in Aigburth. Just far enough out of the city she said so you don't feel the grime. She had a daughter, Emily. (Another Emily he thought.) Sixteen and hoping to become a nurse herself when her schooling was over.

He took special pains to tell Florence how he knew no-one in the city, had no money, no prospects and nowhere to go other than the workhouse, assuming they would take him, when he was discharged. He didn't push it or force the issue; he just let all these things be known. Even languishing in a hospital bed his ability to

57

charm had not deserted him. Let's tell it like was, it was a cynical charm, a shallow charm, but all he cared about was whether it worked or not. Mostly it did. He spoke words of love. Of devotion. As you have nowhere to go she said one morning, I can provide a room for you. All above board mind, I have Emily to consider and my neighbours. We can agree a fair rent when you find yourself a job. Thank you, Florence, you will not regret your decision. You are an angel.

The nightmares started at that time. The beating was replayed over and over. Each time he awoke he has the feeling he has forgotten something; there was something different about the dream each time. The one thing he never forgot whether awake or not was the face of the one who gave the order to assault him. Not just the face, but the voice too. Florence's house was a typical, cramped terrace house although it had the saving grace of overlooking the park. His room was at the very top of the house, which had belonged to Florence's late husband's parents. She and Emily lived frugally not that they had any choice in the matter. It took him a whole two weeks to gravitate from his bed to Florence's bed. The usual inadequacies he felt when it came to relations with a woman were tempered by the fact that Florence had low expectations in that quarter. Expectations that he could meet admirably.

Emily was a strange girl being both surly and uncommunicative. She had no views on this stranger who shared her mother's bed. She had a hint of wildness too, an untamed quality which she wore like a cloak. Her mother despaired of the crowd she ran around with, but was determined to let her live her own life without undue interference. And he wasn't about to interfere himself.

In spite of the unemployment rife in the area he found himself a job. A family run butchers which was a short walk across Sefton Park. Poor wages, poor conditions, but it was work and for now he was satisfied. For now. He had money that was true and he did not feel the need to part with any of his money to Florence. After all, he was her lover not her lodger. And while he professed lover for her and to her he did not feel it. Never had, never will. Throughout his life he had this selfish streak that ran through him. He simply did not care about other people; it was an emotion that he could not comprehend. He looked after himself. Sefton Park came alive at night in a low, mean way that those who traversed its greenery by day would not understand. Courting couples made use of its hidden places as did the local whores. The groans of those who coupled could be heard all over the park. Gangs operated here too as well as sneak thieves. The police made regular patrols, but did little to thwart the lawlessness that pervaded the area. When darkness fell, morals fell too. His confidence was still shaken from his beating, his nerves still on edge. But any fear he felt was alleviated by the comfort of the knives that were sitting in his deep coat pocket. Stolen from the store room at the butcher's. He knew that they would be missed eventually, but when that time came he would simply move on. The comfort and pure pleasure he derived from caressing the bone-handles, from running his finger carefully along the blades was immeasurable. Emily came into view in the dim light of one evening. Accompanying her was a tall man although stoutish. No harm in following them he thought. They found a corner of the park to themselves. Emily was no novice he was certain of that, she was in control. And the two of them together had stamina. He had achieved his own climax long before their incessant fucking had come to an end. He crept away silently, as sated as they were. Even Florence's low expectations would be met that night.

I saw you last night he said. Saw me? Saw me where? In the park. I often come home across the park. I saw you with a man. I saw what you did with that man. What? You were spying on me? Don't be indignant, you were in a public place after all. Perhaps I was concerned for your welfare, Emily he said. How long were you there for? Until the end. Have you told my mother? No. Do you intend to tell my mother? No. But I have a proposal for you.

Sinners buy silence. Emily bought his silence. In his time-honoured tradition. Whore.

SIXTEEN-TWO

As chance had it I met up again with the 'pensioner'. I mentioned him a short while ago if you recall, met him in Windsor. Edward was his name, Edward Stanley. He worked as a brickie or a brickie's mate one of the two. Lived in Osborn Street, but it was rare for me to go there, can't tell you why. I don't mean I won't tell you, I simply mean I don't know. We always spent the weekends together at Crossingham's, old Donovan didn't seem to care, all he had to do as the deputy was to see the money came in. Eddy always paid for my bed those weekends and sometimes he would pay for Eliza's. Rum woman she was, had designs on Eddy, but he was oblivious to it I think. At least I didn't have to find money on a Saturday so I reckoned I could put up with a bit of arguing here and there. I ran into Fountain in the middle of Commercial Road, at least he tolerated me unlike my sisters. He gave me two shillings, personally I think it was easier for him to hand over cash than actually spending time with me not that I was much bothered by that, I was never big on kith and kin, not with my kith and kin anyway. Still, the money came in handy that week was because Eddy was away; he never did tell me where he went. Eliza Cooper was picking fights with me all the time, telling tales about me. First off she tells everyone that Eddy has left me for her and what nonsense that is. Then she accuses me of trying to cheat Harry the Hawker out of a florin. Let me tell you, I wouldn't have dared, that Harry was sharp in spite of how he looked which was kind of slow you know. Caused a right rumpus in the Britannia that did what with Eliza throwing a punch at me and all. She did it

61

again at Crossingham's too and blackened my eye; John Evans who was the night watchman had to step in between us and got a slap for his trouble from her. Bruised my chest too and that didn't help my breathing any I can tell you. Amelia was shocked when I showed her, mind you Eliza didn't get off scot-free. With no sign of Eddy returning I had to get some readies from somewhere and I had the idea of seeing one of my hated sisters and scrounging a little from her, maybe make her feel guilty for all the bad feeling. Best I could do was pick up 5d and then as it was too early to go back to the lodgings I spent it in the Bricklayers; medicinal, better than the medicine I got at the casual ward leastwise. I was in the kitchen at Crossingham's having a beer with old Fred and I kept telling myself, come on girl pull yourself together, if you want a bed for the night you've got to get back out there. I didn't have the strength to go out to Stratford, I barely had the strength to leave the lodging house, but I told Donovan not to let my bed and I would be back before long with the cash. I returned empty-handed and Donovan sent John to collect my bed money which put me in another fix. They didn't seem to care that I was ill; I was just another tart who couldn't cough up her money. That bloody Tim even said that how come I could find money for beer and not for my bed. Easy for him to say that with his bloody easy life. Right, boys I'm off I said, keep that bed for me whatever you do. I thought there may be pickings at Spitalfields market, but there was nothing doing there. I spotted a man on the corner of Hanbury Street who seemed in no particular hurry to be gone. Will you he said and I said yes. Very nearly my last word on this earth. But a few minutes later I said no and it was already too late.

DETRITUS

Long black figured coat.

Black skirt.

Brown bodice.

Another bodice.

Two petticoats.

A large pocket worn under the skirt and tied about the waist with strings (empty when found).

Lace up boots.

Red and white striped woolen stockings.

Neckerchief, white with a wide red border.

Had three recently acquired brass rings on her middle finger.

Scrap of muslin.

One small tooth comb.

One comb in a paper case.

Scrap of envelope.

SEVENTEEN

The excitement and yes, the danger Emily afforded him soon lost its appeal. The control he had over her could not last, he knew that. And as time went on it seemed to him that it was Emily who was exercising the control. In pursuit of respectability Florence had decreed that they should marry and as he could not suggest an alternative he went through with it. What was it after all? A piece of paper, a few words. And life went on as before. Liverpool was his new beginning, a new chapter which opened his new life and the reality was that it was no different to his old life. There were incidental pleasures along the way of course. Whatever hopes he had harboured, whatever expectations he had were spent, carried away on the winds that blew around his dull existence. He had moved from menial job to menial job. His life revolved around butchery, pilfering, trysts with Emily and his deadly dull marriage with Florence. And worst of all he had no idea how to break the cycle. His ever present inner demons were making themselves apparent all the more; his life seemed ready to spiral out of control. It's a wonder he could exist at all in the banal everyday life of his. Nothing satisfied him, he was restless. He wanted change, was desperate for change yet none came. The fault was in him he knew that. As much as he craved something better his own apathy got in the way, when it came down to it, he was just too damn to go out and search for opportunities, for openings, he was content deep down within him to settle for what he had yet the paradox of course was that he did not want to settle. He had never a wanted a family scarred as he was by his own family experiences, yet here he was saddled with a family who afforded him scant pleasures.

His drinking became heavier, his absences from the house longer. The areas of Liverpool he chose to drink in were the roughest, although whole swathes of the city be could described that way. The gangs were hard at their 'work' their rivalries and violence not just directed at themselves, but any unfortunates who happened to get caught up as they went about their daily business. He still had a swelling, slight as it was, to remind him of the casual thuggery. To garner some excitement he joined one of the more notorious gangs, The High-Rips, who patrolled the dock seeking their victims from the masses who were employed there. Unusually for the groups who operated in the city, their crimes were well planned and executed, but with the same level of violence. He became an accepted face, one of the 'boys' although that did not exclude him from the occasional near beating when the High-Rips were perceived as overstepping their boundary. All gangs had their own turf and battles between factions were often about territory, the loss and gain of.

It was in the aftermath of such a battle that he saw a familiar face and heard a familiar voice. It had been some time, but this was the man who had bossed the gang of Cornermen who had attacked him. It was a simple thing to lure him into that alley. A simple thing to appeal to his greed. And a simple thing to gain his revenge. He wanted him to know who he was and why he was punishing him. He wanted to hurt him yes, he wanted to scare him. And when this piece of low-life slumped to his knees after being struck with the handle of his knife, he was possessed by a rage that he could not control nor did he wish to. The blade was sharp, he took great pride in his knives being so, and opened up his throat in one smooth action. When the blood gushed he felt a thrill of vicarious pleasure such as he had never known. His voyeuristic thrills did not compare with this feeling which overwhelmed him utterly. This was real power, real control. The power over life and death.

Now he was faced with a practical problem. Namely, he had to escape, to clear out. It would not take long for witnesses to come forward, for the links to be made. He packed a bag hurriedly. A bag, yes, that's all he had in the world, just enough meagre possessions to fill one bag. And some of Florence's and Emily's possessions too, trinkets and the like that he may be able to pawn. He left a note for Florence which would play havoc with her relationship with her daughter and slammed the door behind him. A part of his life that was over.

He would disappear back into the cess pit that was London, let them look all the wanted, he would not be found. The dark alleys and streets will take their returning son and cover his tracks with impenetrable shadows. He belonged there; he knew that now for certain. He was going home.

EIGHTEEN-THREE

We didn't last long after that, me and John. We were always ill through one thing or another and there was no point in being miserable together so we drifted apart, him back to Poplar and me to lodging houses, work houses and various beds. I had to go cap in hand back to the Swedish church for more hand outs and I thought of a tale to tell which was bound to put a little money my way. It's like this I said, my poor husband and my babies were drowned on the Princess Alice. He fought hard to save them and died manfully. I was kicked in the mouth as I tried to reach my youngest and I only came round when the cold water revived me. Here, I sobbed while they looked on, taking their notes. If only I had stayed in Sweden I screamed. They nodded and after ten minutes of whispering amongst themselves I got my money. You are welcome to say, what a dreadful thing to invent, what a wicked woman you are, but I say, put yourself in my boots. As it happens, I don't think Sven Olsson who was the clerk of the church and the head of the alms committee believed my story, but who cares about that, the money was mine. Not that it amounted to much. But don't think me ungrateful please. I met Michael round about that time. He was younger than me and I took to him straight away. He had a place in Devonshire Street and we lived there together although I would often go off from time to time and come back to him when it suited. He didn't like my drinking or the company I kept. He even tried to lock me in to keep me out of the pubs. I wasn't about to stand for that now was I? Even came to blows and I had him charged although he begged me not to go through with it, said he would change, don't all men. I let it drop anyway and just didn't turn up at court. I was no stranger to the court mind you, eight times I was up there, drunk and disorderly they said, but what the hell harm was I doing? None to anyone, but me. Your English courts are always slanted against foreigners, you see us as heathens I think. There was a policeman I knew who would point me in the direction of home wherever that might be at the time and send me on my way, but others would drag you off to the cells kicking and screaming. Sometimes when I was released I would go back to Michael, but he was often as drunk as I was. So much for his protective ways. I had a flaming row with him; I forget what it was about, probably money. I had been making some decent money with my charring and cleaning. Not decent money as the likes of you might make, but good enough for me. Rack my brains as I might I don't know why we argued, it was either money or drink so let's just say it was one of those shall we? I got out and left him to cool down and headed to the doss house in Flower and Dean Street. On the way I met an old friend and we agreed to meet at the Bricklayers Arms the following evening. He was just a friend I knew from Stepney way although I was sure I had seen him recently in Dorset Street, nothing had gone on between us, but he was a nice enough fellow, good looking and charming. Tried to look my best for him, put on my nicest clothes and then found I had lost my hair brush. Would you believe it? No one at the house would let me borrow theirs. Still, it was windy and wet so I dare say it would have made no difference anyway. We had a few drinks at the Bricklayers and he was quite amorous which was odd because he had never been that way with me before. I didn't object mind. Like I said, he was a nice fellow. When I agreed to go with him if you know what I mean, he said you would say yes to anything and say anything apart from your prayers. Do I need to say my prayers then I replied. Yes Liz I'm afraid you do he said with a smile.

68

DETRITUS

Long black cloth jacket, fur trimmed around the bottom with a red rose and white maiden hair fern pinned to it. (She was not wearing the flowers when she left the lodging house.).

Black skirt.

Black crepe bonnet.

Checked neck scarf knotted on left side.

Dark brown velveteen bodice.

2 light serge petticoats.

1 white chemise.

White stockings.

Spring sided boots.

2 handkerchiefs (one, the larger, is noticed at the post-mortem to have fruit stains on it.).

A thimble.

A piece of wool wound around a card.

A key (as of a padlock).

A small piece of lead pencil.

Six large and one small button.

A comb.

A broken piece of comb.

A metal spoon.

A hook (as from a dress).

A piece of muslin.

One or two small pieces of paper.

A packet of Cachous.

DEFINITIONS

Jack London: The People of the Abyss: Whitechapel in 1902

In the last twelve years, one district, "London over the Border," as it is called, which lies well beyond Aldgate, Whitechapel, and Mile End, has increased 260,000 or over sixty percent. The churches in this district, by the way, can seat but one in every thirty-seven of the added population. The City of Dreadful Monotony the East End is often called, especially by well-fed, optimistic sightseers, who look over the surface of things and are merely shocked by the intolerable sameness and meanness of it all. If the East End is worthy of no worse title than The City of Dreadful Monotony, and if working people are unworthy of variety and beauty and surprise, it would not be such a bad place in which to live. But the East End does merit a worse title. It should be called The City of Degradation. While it is not a city of slums, as some people imagine, it may well be said to be one gigantic slum. From the standpoint of simple decency and clean manhood and womanhood, any mean street, of all its mean streets, is a slum. Where sights and sounds abound which neither you nor I would care to have our children see and hear is a place where no man's children should live and see and hear. Where you and I would not care to have our wives pass their lives is a place where no other man's wife should have to pass her life. For here, in the East End, the obscenities and brute vulgarities of life are rampant. There is no privacy. The bad corrupts the good, and all fester together.

NINETEEN

Home. The East End was the perfect place to lose himself in, one more lost soul amongst so many. The money he had left was enough for a room for a few days while he looked for work. It was home, yet he believed himself to be much better than those who lived and worked around him. He had intelligence which no one used, he had learning which was not required. He had brains which were scarcely necessary. He had cunning which at least gave him a chance to rise above the degradation which engulfed him. But he did not rise. There was nothing about his life that set him apart in any way from the folk who teemed around him, their sad, pathetic lives which mirrored his own. The work was easy to find, his skills with knives would always be in demand. Not that it made any difference in the wages he received. They covered his money for his bed and for food and drink. But what else did he need? The money he obtained dishonestly did no more than his wages did except it kept him in drink longer. Whitechapel very quickly became both home and prison.

And he had killed a man in cold blood, he could not forget that. Did not want to forget it. He relived the moment so many times, had slit his throat over and over so many times. The memories became sweeter each time, the crimson tide of blood more vivid each time. He knew it would happen again, had to happen again. He was no stranger to urges. Some he resisted, some he gave into. Whores.

The underbelly of London became his patch. The pubs of the East End became his places of worship. The Bricklayer's Arms, The Six Bells, The Golden Lion, The Lamb, The Bull. He absolved himself in them daily, only leaving them when his devotions were over and the reality of work took over. He became nocturnal, a creature of the night, going where he wished at will, no one giving him a second glance. His nighttime perambulations became a mandatory routine, one he could not live without. Tramping the streets until the clock struck five and then knives jangling in his inner pocket would retrace his steps to Dorset Street to Cohen the butcher who depended on him, but would rather do without him if he could. That was his impression anyway. And his impressions could usually be relied on.

He was a part of the fabric of Whitechapel, few knew his name, even fewer could claim to be his friend. There was, as there always had been, something that set him apart, something which did not invite any form of intimacy. Which suited him perfectly. The time he spent with prostitutes was perfunctory with their hurried almost shameful couplings that he came to hate although, yes, they satisfied a need in him. The disgust he felt for these creatures was overbearing. He hated them even at the moment of his using them. They knew his weakness. They recognised it in him. At times he could not be sure that he hated them more than he hated himself.

After one unsatisfactory visit (were not all of them so he thought) a necessary visit to a local doctor confirmed what he was dreading. He had caught the pox, the clap, whatever you wanted to call it. It was a fact of life in the East End if not a way of life, but he had never encountered anything quite so shameful. Had never been so ashamed, so unclean. He shunned the pubs, he shunned work. He brooded. There was only one whore of late and he would know her again. He knew the area she could be found. He even

73

knew her name; Polly. She would have to pay when he found her amongst this struggling humanity that surrounded him.

Polly Nichols. There she was. What a sight she was, she could hardly stand up. He had to help her, what a laugh that was. She recognised him at the last moment, at least he thought so. She paid her debt in full. He was under control the whole time. He was pleased about that. To be in the grip of a rage and to be in control, now that was a trick few could achieve he thought. He walked home to Dorset Street through the pouring rain, satisfied in every conceivable way with his night's work. Satisfied, but oddly unfulfilled.

He knew the answer to that however. His killing days were not over, in fact they had hardly begun.

TWENTY-FOUR

That last trudge back to London took forever; I had never been so
tired. Yes, I know what I said about being made of strong stuff,
but I still say I was entitled to feel as I felt then. John managed to
earn 6d so he went off to Cooney's. It was 4d a night there so it
was impossible to both stay there, but I knew I could get a bed at
the casual ward in Shoe Lane and 2d would see me right for a cup
of char and a bite to eat. Got myself in a spot of bother in the ward
for arguing with the superintendent there. He was just too fond of
poking his nose into my business and I told him a few home truths
which very quickly got me chucked out. At least I had managed to
get some sleep. Walked across to Cooney's and persuaded Johnny
to pawn his last decent pair of boots. 2/6d we got for them, plenty
enough to get some bread, milk, tea and sugar. It wasn't much of a
breakfast that's for sure, but I was ravenous and didn't care. By
the time we had been to the Red Lion there was no money left so I
decided to go to Annie's in Bermondsey to see what I could cadge
there or I would be sleeping God knows where. My own flesh and
blood, but she couldn't wait to send me on my way, it's like I was
a stranger rather than her mother. Still, she gave me a shilling, a
whole shilling. Never made it back to Clooney's although I
remember I was heading in that direction. Lord knows how I
ended up in Aldgate in the state I was and what a state. I vaguely
recall falling down and being helped up by a policeman of all
people. Next thing I know I am in a cell in Bishopsgate police
station. What's your name someone asks. No idea I said. Cell door
slammed shut. I was feeling a bit more like it later and asked when

I would be let out. Depends when you are capable of looking after yourself he said. I reckoned I was more than capable and told him so. Out you come he said a while later. What time is it? Too late for you to get anything to drink. I shall get a damn fine hiding when I get home. Serves you right, you had no right to get drunk. This way missus, please pull the door to. All right, good night old cock. I had to lean against the wall for a while and get my bearings and clear my head a little. Had no right to get drunk! Bloody policeman, why are they preaching to me instead of catching this murdering madman? I think I was on Houndsditch when I fell in step with a man who seemed as drunk as me. Shortish, flushed even excited. Must be the drink I thought. We ended up walking, well, more like staggering down Church Passage. Have you money then I asked. He flashed me some coins. 6d for you matey how does that sound? He just nodded. I knew that's why you brought me down here you know. Did you, how? Because it's a dead end I replied. It certainly is. The deadest end you will ever know.

DETRITUS

Black straw bonnet trimmed in green and black velvet with black beads. Black strings, worn tied to the head.

Black cloth jacket trimmed around the collar and cuffs with imitation fur and around the pockets in black silk braid and fur. Large metal buttons.

Dark green chintz skirt, 3 flounces, brown button on waistband. Man's white vest, matching buttons down front.

Brown linsey bodice, black velvet collar with brown buttons down front.

Grey stuff petticoat with white waistband.

Very old green alpaca skirt.

Very old ragged blue skirt with red flounces, light twill.

White calico chemise.

Pair of men's lace up boots, mohair laces. Right boot repaired with red thread.

1 piece of red gauze silk worn as a neckerchief.

1 large white pocket handkerchief.

1 large white cotton handkerchief with red and white bird's eye border.

2 unbleached calico pockets, tape strings.

1 blue stripe bed ticking pocket.

Brown ribbed knee stockings, darned at the feet with white cotton.

2 small blue bags made of bed ticking

2 short black clay pipes.

1 tin box containing tea.

1 tin box containing sugar.

1 tin matchbox, empty.

12 pieces white rag, some slightly bloodstained.

1 piece coarse linen, white.

1 piece of blue and white shirting, 3 cornered.

1 piece red flannel with pins and needles.

6 pieces soap.

1 small tooth comb.

1 white handle table knife.

1 metal teaspoon.

1 red leather cigarette case with white metal fittings.

1 ball hemp.

1 piece of old white apron with repair.

Several buttons and a thimble.

Mustard tin containing two pawn tickets.

Printed handbill.

Portion of a pair of spectacles.

1 red mitten.

Where are you going? Do you know where you are going? Where are you running to? Can you run? Do you think you can hide? Where can you hide? Have you nothing to say to us? What can you say? Where will you go? Where can you go? Can you hear us? Can you hear what we say? And you have nothing to say to us? Nothing at all? Are you scared? How scared are you? Is your heart pounding? How fast is it pounding? What can you hear? Can you hear a rushing? Is it the river you can hear? How does fear feel? Can you tell us? What are you thinking now? Are you thinking? Are you praying? What are you praying? Is your breathing difficult? How difficult is it? Are you gasping for air? Who can save you? Can anybody save you? Can you be saved? Does it feel like drowning? Are you drowning?

Not yet.

DEFINITIONS

psychopath psy·cho·path (sī'kə-pāth')

noun.

A person with an antisocial personality disorder, especially one manifested in perverted, criminal, or amoral behaviour.

Also called: sociopath, a person afflicted with a personality disorder characterized by a tendency to commit antisocial and sometimes violent acts and a failure to feel guilt for such acts.

TWENTY-ONE

The hue and cry for the killer was not as great as he imagined it would be. Although the endemic violence of the area was well known, it tended to be of a casual nature and murders were actually quite rare. He kept to his usual routine; boarding house (a new one now: on Thrawl Street), nocturnal wanderings and his work. He was not about to change any part of his life. He was adept at not being caught. Hide in plain sight he thought. Here I am come and catch me. But they won't.

He was standing on the corner of Hanbury Street. He had no idea why he was loitering there. He had broken his own rule in the matter of routine for he should have been at the butcher's by then. Fate? Maybe he thought. He was approached by a destitute looking character. Will you he asked. Yes was the answer. It was never going to be anything else. No struggle. No alarm. And time to do as he wished. He was methodical as he was thorough. Dispassionate and determined. He almost lingered too long admiring his handicraft; he would not make that mistake again.

He had not had the opportunity to wash the blood of his hands before arriving at Cohen's. Started without us have you asked John. He was startled for a moment, but responded with a comment which seemed to satisfy. The body would be discovered soon and the hunt on. If John heard and remembered, but he need not worry too much. John was slow-witted and lived in a world of his own. He had no worries there. And if he did, there would be more work for his knife to do. It was all over Whitechapel a couple of days later that there had been an arrest. A shoe-maker by the name of Jack Pizer. God only knows why the police picked on him. Laughable really. And far worse than that, he did not want anyone else to take the credit for his crimes. They belonged to him; they bore the signs of his artistry. How dare the police pick on simpletons and imagine them to have his mastery. They would have to learn along with everyone else.

Fate played a part once more. He came across a woman he knew from his time in Stepney. Lucky Liz was how he knew her. Although her luck had started to run out. Poor wretch. He arranged to meet her at the Bricklayer's Arms. He did not consider himself to be taking any kind of chance. He had certainly not decided on Liz's fate. His only worry afterwards was being recognised for he was no stranger to the Bricklayer's even though he had always been as anonymous as he could be, sitting in quiet corners, leaning against walls in the shadows. During the course of that interminable evening, when Liz made it clear what she wanted from him, no doubt in return for her bed money, his mood darkened and he knew what fate had in store for Unlucky Liz. He suggested she say her prayers. She would have need of them. Damn that horse and that little man. He had no time to finish the job. Barely suppressing his anger he fled the square into the darkness. He knew the alleys well and was confident he would not be tracked down. The body would have been found at once he thought. His anger at the interruption to his work ate away at him as he twisted and turned the lanes. He found himself in Houndsditch. For the first time he experienced the pangs of a loss of control. It was not where he expected to be or where he wanted to be. There was a woman ahead of him, drunk and unsteady. And alone. She assumed him to be as drunk as she was, mistaking his combination of anger and rising excitement for intoxication. Church Passage was a few steps away. It would be dark, quiet. It was a dead end. Deader than ever that night. This time he could linger, he could tarry. He took his time, making every incision count. An artist, once more in control.

The man-hunt was on. The police presence doubled, tripled. Bloodhounds in the streets. Rewards offered. People stopped and searched. Likenesses of suspects printed in the newspapers. He had to admit, one or two looked very much like him to the smallest detail, but still he came and went without hindrance. He had always thought they would never catch him, they had no earthly hope of doing do. He would go on killing for as long as he wanted. This power over life and death was not about to be taken away from him. However, he counted himself a sensible man and took what precautions he could. He would wait awhile before selecting his next victim. And if the streets were still full of policemen running around chasing their own shadows then he would had to make alternative plans.

He waited a month, a long month. It was not a fully conscious decision for he had recognised the virtue of patience. The truth was that opportunities had been scarce. The whole populace was on their guard against this madman in their midst. How dare they combine to stop him? He never allowed his frustration to boil over, he daren't lose control. All the same, he felt himself reaching a kind of boiling-point.

He knew her by sight if not by name. Lived in Miller's Court, an unsavoury place if ever there was one. A few yards away from where he lived himself. He was back in Dorset Street, that street of ill-reputation. He stood in the shadows and listened to her conversation with George Hutchinson. He knew him alright. A good for nothing sort of man. She asked him for money and he span a tale of not having any. She believed him and said she would get some. On an impulse he stepped forward and offered her a shilling not that he any intention of parting with it. He was wary, this was very close to home, but after a month he was willing to take the risk. She died quickly, quietly. And then his long delayed work started. The hovel was so dark he had to light a fire so he could see the wounds he was inflicting on her. He gave full rein to his blood-lust. Demons from hell could learn from him. He barely noticed the girl or thought of her as a person until he was done. Good God, there was nothing left of her he thought. This will make everyone sit up and take notice even more. Look at me he thought, see what I can do. He relished the thought that he was the most talked about man in the country; he had made his mark at last. Everyone knows him. Everyone fears him.

His work would never end. He did not know that it was already over.

TWENTY-TWO-FIVE

If only Joe hadn't lost his job. If only I hadn't had to go back on the streets. Joe hated me tarting myself, but if he had been able to provide for me like a real man then I wouldn't have had to. That makes sense doesn't it? It did to me. He crawled off to Buller's, but he would be back. He even objected to me inviting other unfortunates to share the room like Marie and Julia poor souls. I can get along without you, Joe Barnett I thought. Except he still kept coming back just like I thought. Every day he was there. To see how I was he said. More likely trying to catch me with another man. That last time I had Lizzie with me. She did not care for Joe any more than he did for her so he soon left us alone. I was restless and needed a drink badly. The landlord, old 'Tubby' at the Britannia sometimes let me have a beer for less than the asking price on receipt of certain favours so that's where I headed. Met a lovely bloke there called William who paid for a pail of beer. I took him back to Millers Court, singing all the time. *'Only a violet I plucked when but a boy, And oft' times when I'm sad at heart, this flow'r has given me joy. But while life does remain, in memoriam I'll retain this small violet I plucked from mother's grave'.* I reckon some kind of madness had got into me. I sang and sang like never before. I think everyone in the East End must have heard me! *'Well I remember my dear old mother's smile, as she used to greet me when I returned from toil; always knitting in the old arm chair. Father used to sit and read for all us children there. But now all is silent around the good old home. They all have left me in sorrow here to roam; while life does remain, in*

86

memoriam I'll retain this small violet I plucked from mother's grave.' I cooked us up a dish of fish and a few left over potatoes. He was a generous man in every way, but I daresay he had a wife to go home to so he took his leave saying he would be back one day. Good I said. Mind you, although he was generous I was still in need of money and wanted to try my hand at earning it before Joe returned. I met George Hutchinson in Flower and Dean Street. He was another gent who was kind to me on occasion. Have you got sixpence for poor Mary, Mr Hutchinson? Afraid not he says I spent it all in Romford. In Romford I said, there's a thing. Don't worry I will get some money. Good night Mr Hutchinson. I've got some money for you said a man who stepped out of the shadows. Have you now? He showed me a shiny new shilling. What do you think? I said that will do all right. It will be all right he said, I can tell you that. He seemed a bit shy to tell you the truth and he was a bit wary about coming into the court. Come along I said, I will make you comfortable. Come on, I said again as I kissed him. I put my hand in my sleeve. Damn, I have lost my handkerchief. Here, have this one he said and handed me a bright red one. It looks like it has been dipped in blood I said. Yes it does doesn't it.

IT ALL COMES DOWN TO NUMBERS IN THE END.

370

DAZ 048850

281

HC 084466

479

HC 084467

258

DA 818098

326

HC 08437

He has seen the abyss. It is waiting. Welcoming and inviting.

The voices, now more nagging and insistent propel him forward. His last shreds of resistance are used up. He is resigned, even calm you might say. The steady stream of early morning human traffic crossing the bridge would counter this, for they see a deranged madman in their midst. A man in the throes of uttering a silent scream with hands over his ears, clawing wildly at his hair. They move on quickly, not wishing to play any part in this drama being played out in front of them.

He suddenly stands quite still as if he is only now aware of where he is; the bridge; the abyss.

The voices close in. Whispering at first, now screaming in his ears. He sees shapes forming from out of the London fog.

Nowhere to go. You have nowhere to go. Now tell us how it feels. Tell us. Are you climbing? Where are you climbing? Where do you think you can go? Where can you go? What if lose your grip? What then? What if we make you lose your grip? What then? That's it, stand there. Stand there and perhaps you will be safe. Look at us. Turn your head and look at us. Can you see us? Do you see us? Do you know us? Do you know who we are? LOOK at us!

Dear God in Heaven he sees. The voices no longer mingle, they now belong to their owners who step out of the fog. With a purpose. With a goal. He looks around for escape. There is none. They come closer. All of them. They claw at him as he tries to climb higher onto the bridge. Their nails rake his skin. He stares at them. They are all here now. His mother, Aunt Katherine, Polly Nichols, Annie Chapman, Liz Stride, Catherine Eddowes and Mary Kelly. He kicks out at them.

You can't hurt us anymore. You have lost that power. Climb higher. Go on. Higher. Do it. Do it.

They crawl over the ironwork like elongated malignant spiders, chanting, screaming, goading.

Do it. Do it.

He stands. The wind whipping up his coat. Down below the Thames rolling along. Down below, the abyss begins to open up for him.

Down below, the Thames.

Welcoming.

Receiving.

****

The facts are these:

Jack the Ripper is the best-known name given to an unidentified serial killer who was active in the largely impoverished areas in and around the Whitechapel district of London in 1888. The name originated in a letter, written by someone claiming to be the murderer, that was disseminated in the media. The letter is widely believed to have been a hoax, and may have been written by a journalist in a deliberate attempt to heighten interest in the story. Within the crime case files as well as journalistic accounts the killer was known as "the Whitechapel Murderer" as well as "Leather Apron".

Attacks ascribed to the Ripper typically involved female prostitutes who lived and worked in the slums of London and whose throats were cut prior to abdominal mutilations. The removal of internal organs from at least three of the victims led to proposals that their killer possessed anatomical or surgical knowledge. Rumours that the murders were connected intensified in September and October 1888, and letters from a writer or writers purporting to be the murderer were received by media outlets and Scotland Yard. The "From Hell" letter, received by George Lusk of the Whitechapel Vigilance Committee, included half of a preserved human kidney, supposedly from one of the victims. Mainly because of the extraordinarily brutal character of the murders, and because of media treatment of the events, the public came increasingly to believe in a single serial killer known as "Jack the Ripper".

There are five generally accepted victims although this itself is a cause for argument. Some commentators only claim four, others upwards of ten. The five so-called 'canonical' victims were:

Mary Ann Nichols (Polly) 31 August 1888

Annie Chapman 8 September 1888

Elizabeth Stride 30 September 1888

Catherine Eddowes 30 September 1888

Mary Kelly 9 November 1888

There was no shortage of suspects at the time and there have been many more put forward since. These include: Prince Albert Victor, Dr. Barnardo, Joseph Barnett)Mary Kelly's lover), Montague John Druitt, James Maybrick, Dr. Cream, James Kelly, Jack Pizer, Lewis Carroll, George Chapman, Walter Sickert, Francis Tumblety and literally hundreds more, often on the flimsiest of evidence.

It all comes down to only one unassailable fact. Just this one fact: And it is this. The identity of Jack the Ripper was will never be known.

Acknowledgements

To Gill, first and foremost, who suggested I write 'something different', well this is my 'something different'.

The most valuable resource available online for budding 'Ripperologists' is www.casebook.org a gold mine of information that I used extensively.

'The Mammoth Book of Jack the Ripper' published by Robinsons of London and edited by Maxim Jakubowski and Nathan Braund is comprehensive and fairly up to date on all aspects of the murders and investigation.

Thanks to Steve at MX and Bob at Staunch for their customary help.

David Ruffle October 2013

Also From MX Publishing

Winners of the 2011 Howlett Literary Award (Sherlock Holmes book of the year) for '**The Norwood Author**'

From one of the world's largest Sherlock Holmes publishers dozens of new novels from the top Holmes authors around the world.

www.mxpublishing.com

Including our bestselling short story collections 'Lost Stories of Sherlock Holmes' and 'The Outstanding Mysteries of Sherlock Holmes'.

Also from David Ruffle

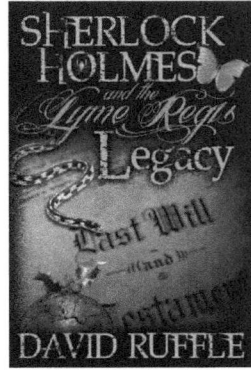

Sherlock Holmes and The Lyme Regis Horror, and the sequels
Sherlock Holmes and The Lyme Regis Legacy and Sherlock
Holmes and The Lyme Regis Trials

Sherlock Holmes – Tales from the Stranger's Room (Vol 1 and 2)
An eclectic collection of writings from twenty Holmes writers.

www.mxpublishing.com

Also from MX Publishing
Sherlock Holmes Travel Guides

London   Devon

And in ebook (stunning on the iPad) an interactive guide to
London

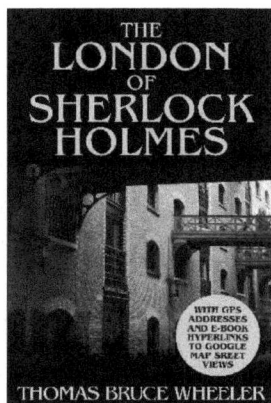

400 locations linked to Google Street View.

Also from MX Publishing
Sherlock Holmes Fiction

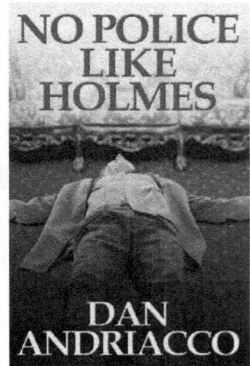

Short fiction (Discarded Cigarette, Russian Chessboard), modern novels (No Police Like Holmes), a female Sherlock Holmes (My Dear Watson) and the adventures of Mrs Watson (Sign of Fear, and Study in Crimson).

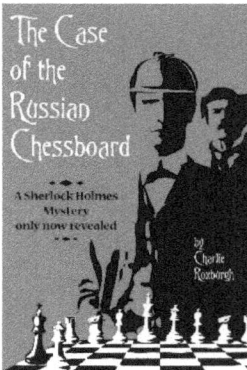

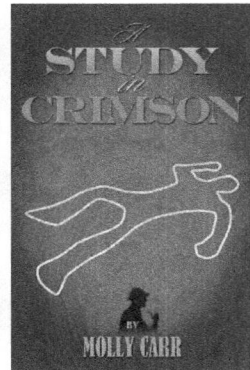

Also from MX Publishing

Biographies of Arthur Conan Doyle

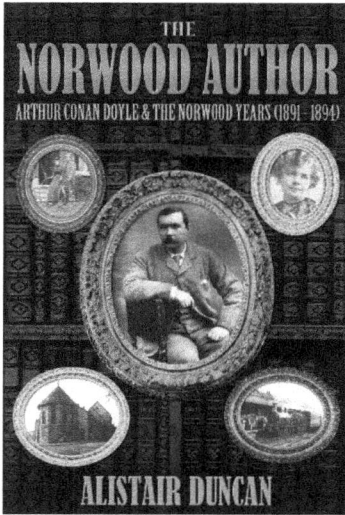

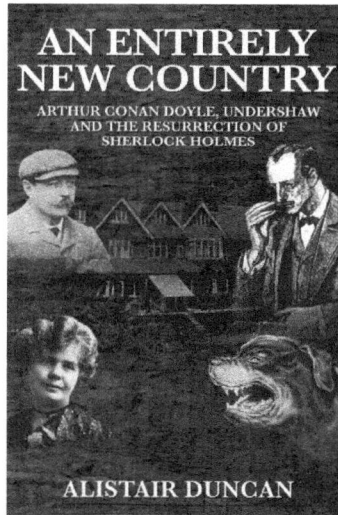

The Norwood Author. Winner of the 2011 Howlett Literary Award (Sherlock Holmes Book of the year) and the most important historical Holmes book of a decade 'An Entirely New Country'.